P9-DTL-512

# THE
# PICTURE STORY
# OF
# REGGIE JACKSON

**Books by George Sullivan**
The Picture Story of Reggie Jackson
The Picture Story of Catfish Hunter
Home Run!
Better Ice Skating for Boys and Girls
The Catcher: Baseball's Man in Charge
Pro Football A to Z
Winning Plays in Pro Football
Hank Aaron
Winning Basketball
The Complete Book of Autograph Collecting
Better Bicycling for Boys and Girls
Baseball's Art of Hitting
The New World of Robots
The Picture Story of Nadia Comaneci

# THE
# PICTURE STORY
## OF
# REGGIE JACKSON

## by George Sullivan

Illustrated with photographs

Julian Messner

New York

Published by Julian Messner, a Simon & Schuster
Division of Gulf & Western Corporation, Simon &
Schuster Building, 1230 Avenue of the Americas,
New York, N.Y. 10020

Copyright © 1977 by George Sullivan

Third Printing, 1978

Printed in the United States of America

Library of Congress Cataloging in Publication Data

Sullivan, George
    The picture story of Reggie Jackson.

    SUMMARY: A biography of the baseball player famous for
his powerful long-distance hitting.
    1. Jackson, Reggie — Juvenile literature. 2. Baseball players —
United States — Biography — Juvenile literature.
[1. Jackson, Reggie. 2. Baseball players. 3. Afro-Americans —
Biography] I. Title.
GV865.J32S94        796.357'092'4 [B] [92]        77-4660
ISBN 0-671-32913-8

## Photo Credits

Cleveland Indians: p. 30

El Delator, Cheltenham (Pa.) High School: pp. 14, 15, 16, 17

Jonathan Perry, Longhair Photography: pp. 6, 10, 28, 38, 42, 46, 47, 51, 52

George Sullivan: pp. 13, 19, 26, 31, 44, 45, 53, 57, 61

United Press International Photos: pp. 9, 22, 24, 25, 33, 34, 35, 37, 40, 54, 59

*Reggie Jackson's home-run swing.*

Reggie Jackson would rather hit a baseball than do just about anything else in the world. When he does hit, he hits hard. He can whack a baseball out of shape.

Take, for example, the 1971 All-Star game, which was played on a warm July night at Tiger Stadium in Detroit. Reggie didn't think that he would be named to the All-Star team that season. He was only 25 then, a member of the Oakland Athletics, a team that had never won so much as a division title. But when Minnesota's Tony Oliva was unable to play, Reggie was called upon to substitute, even though there were many other outfielders better known than he was.

Pittsburgh's Dock Ellis was pitching for the National Leaguers, who were ahead, 3-0, after two innings. Ellis gave up a single to Boston's Luis Aparicio, leading off in the third. Reggie, a left-handed hitter, came to the plate. The count went to one-and-two. Reggie flicked his bat back and forth, eyeing the pitcher carefully.

Ellis checked the runner at first, then fired a steaming fastball. Reggie whipped his bat around, felt it make contact, then watched the ball rocket toward right-center field, rising as it traveled. At first, Reggie thought the ball was going to land in the upper stands, but it kept soaring and finally cleared the roof to strike at the base of a tall light tower. The crowd oohed and aahed. The blow was the longest home run in the history of the All-Star game, and one of the few balls ever hit over the roof at Tiger Stadium.

Reggie's tremendous smash gave the American League team a much needed boost. Two outs later, Frank Robinson of the Baltimore Orioles knocked an Ellis pitch into the lower stands in right field with a runner on base. The American Leaguers eventually won, 6-3, ending an eight-game losing streak.

Afterward, everyone talked about the ball that Reggie hit. "He crushed it," said slugger Frank Howard of the Washington Senators. "You don't see five balls hit like that in a lifetime." Detroit's Al Kaline, whose exceptional career had spanned eighteen seasons, called it, "The hardest hit ball I've ever seen in my life."

Few baseball players do as many things as

*A smiling Don Buford congratulates Reggie after his All-Star home run in 1971.*

well as Reggie Jackson. Besides hitting the ball hard, his arm is one of the best in baseball. And he runs with surprising speed on the bases.

Reggie's chief asset is his strength. He is 6 feet tall, and weighs 204 pounds. His arms and thighs bulge with muscles.

*Jackson excels on the basepaths, too.*

Even as a youngster, Reggie was husky and powerful. He was born in Wyncote, Pennsylvania, on May 18, 1946, and brought up in nearby Cheltenham. Both are small towns just north of Philadelphia.

Reggie's full name is Reginald Martinez Jackson. He was named Reginald after the doctor who delivered him. Martinez is his father's first name. "We're black," says Reggie, "but my father's people came from Latin America."

There were six children in the Jackson family. Reggie had two older brothers, Joe and Jim, and an older sister, Dolores. He had two younger sisters, Beverly and Tina.

When Reggie was four years old, his parents separated. Reggie, Joe and Beverly went to live with their father. The other children went with their mother. Mr. and Mrs. Jackson were later divorced.

Mr. Jackson, a tailor, ran a clothes dry cleaning shop. He left for work at daybreak and did not return until very late at night. Young Reggie had to make his own breakfast and get to school by himself. Whenever he wanted pocket money, he had to earn it. His father would put him to work delivering dry cleaning to his customers. When he was older, Reggie operated the pressing machine in his father's shop. The steam from the machine made it hot work, and he didn't like it.

Reggie was raised in a neighborhood in which race was not an important factor. "My father didn't know what 'color' was," says Reggie, "and he still doesn't."

His father's attitude influenced Reggie. "I wouldn't know what color I was if Whites didn't make me feel black and Blacks didn't make me feel blacker," he says.

"I'm proud to be black," Reggie adds. "I don't want to be white. But I don't see color. I'm a man first. I don't like people to say, 'I'm a black man first or white first.' That emphasizes the differences. We are the same underneath."

Reggie was always interested in sports. Almost everyday, he, his brother Joe, and their friends played softball or football on an empty lot behind Mr. Jackson's cleaning shop.

Willie Mays and Hank Aaron were among Reggie's boyhood heroes. They were his favorites because each one had so many different skills. "They could beat you in a lot of ways," Reggie says. Later, when he became a major leaguer, some of his teammates called him "Buck," be-

*The great Willie Mays, one of Reggie's idols.*

cause that had been Willie Mays' nickname, and they knew how much he admired Mays.

In the fall of 1960, Reggie entered Cheltenham High School. There he was to lead in every sport he tried.

*In high school, Reggie was a running back, and won the team's MVP award as a senior.*

Football was his best sport. He was a running back, and liked the physical contact that football offered. Once, during a game, a defensive line-man hit Reggie in the mouth, breaking one of his teeth. Reggie boiled with anger. He asked his quarterback to call a play in which he would carry the ball. Taking the quarterback's hand-off,

Reggie went barreling for the lineman, knocking him to the ground.

Reggie also played defensive halfback on the team. "When you've got a player as talented as Reggie was," one of his coaches recalls, "you use him as much as you can."

In three seasons as a running back, Reggie averaged eight yards per carry and scored 30 touchdowns. He won the school's Holden Award which was given to the team's most valuable player. Reggie's high school yearbook predicted that he was to become a football all-American.

*Reggie's high school yearbook forecast him as a "future all-American."*

On the high school baseball team, Reggie was a pitcher, a fastballing left-hander. When he wasn't assigned to pitch, he played first base. "You couldn't afford to let someone with his power at the plate sit on the bench," his coach recalls. In his senior year, Reggie hurled three no hitters for the Cheltenham Panthers and batted .550.

*Reggie scores a run for the Cheltenham Panthers.*

*Between baseball and football seasons, Reggie (No. 56) starred for the high school basketball team.*

In between football and baseball seasons, Reggie played for the basketball team. He was a forward with a good outside shot, and he liked to mix it up on the boards. Reggie also managed to go out for track. He would sometimes show up for track practice still wearing his baseball uniform. He didn't have time to change.

Impressed with Reggie's athletic ability, many colleges offered him scholarships. Reggie chose Arizona State University in Tempe, Arizona.

He continued to star as a running back. But during his freshman year, when he suffered a leg injury, the coach said he couldn't be a runner any more, and moved him into the defensive backfield. Reggie didn't like being on the defensive team only. He wasn't in the spotlight enough.

One day, a teammate bet Reggie five dollars that he couldn't make the ASU baseball team, one of the finest college teams in the nation. In those days five dollars meant a great deal to Reggie, so he made the bet.

Reggie went to Bobby Winkles, the baseball coach, and asked him if he could take batting practice with the team. "Sure," said Winkles. When Reggie blasted a couple of pitches over the fence, Winkles urged him to try out for the team. "I really wasn't interested in making the team," says Reggie. "I was a football player. But there was that bet I wanted to win."

Reggie became the regular center fielder for the Arizona State freshman team, and won the bet. When the college season was over, Winkles arranged for him to get some more training during the summer with a top-rated semipro team in Baltimore, Maryland, known as Leone's-Johnny's. "He was still more of a football player than a

*Bobby Winkles, manager of the Arizona State baseball team, was later to join Reggie as a coach for the A's.*

baseball player," says Walter Youse, the team's manager. "He had a lot of rough edges. But he wanted to learn and he worked hard. He came early; he stayed late."

Reggie liked being in Baltimore. His mother and his sisters now lived there, and he saw them frequently.

Reggie returned to college in the fall and played for the varsity football team. The next spring he starred for the varsity baseball team, leading in runs batted in, runs scored, hits, and stolen bases. He belted 15 home runs, a school record. He once hit a home run out of Phoenix Memorial Stadium, something no other college player had ever done.

Reggie's hitting feats came to the attention of Charles O. Finley, owner of the Kansas City Athletics. Finley told Reggie he would pay him a bonus if he would quit college and sign with the A's. Finley opened with an offer of $60,000. When he got to $95,000, Reggie signed.

The A's assigned Reggie to their Lewiston (Idaho) club in the Northwest League. He stayed there only a few weeks before moving up the ladder to Modesto (California) in the California League. Although he played in only 56 games for the Modesto team, Reggie hit 21 home runs and was named the league's Player of the Year. This earned him a promotion to Birmingham (Alabama) of the Southern Association for the 1967 season.

Willie Mays had been born and brought up on the outskirts of Birmingham, and played his first professional baseball there at the age of 16 for the Birmingham Black Barons. When it was announced that Reggie had been assigned to the A's Birmingham farm team, a local newspaper featured a full page of photographs and stories about him. The page carried the headline: REMEMBER WILLIE MAYS?; MEET REGGIE JACKSON.

Reggie impressed everyone in Birmingham with his power and speed. He hit 17 homers, batted .293, and led the league in triples and runs scored. Again he was chosen Player of the Year. Late in the season, he was promoted to the A's roster, and played 35 games for the team.

The Athletics moved from Kansas City to Oakland, California, in 1968. They were a young team. Reggie Jackson, 21 years old that spring, was the youngest member of all.

Bob Kennedy, the A's manager, described Reggie as having "God-given gifts." But he was still lacking in experience, and like any inexperienced player, he made mistakes. During the exhibition season, he would sometimes misjudge fly balls or throw to the wrong base. In one game, he dropped a line drive for one error, then kicked the ball around for another. Meanwhile, the runners raced around the bases. Another time, Reggie stumbled and fell while trying to stretch a single into a double, and was out by a mile. But Kennedy stuck with him and made Reggie the A's regular right fielder. Kennedy realized that Jackson had all the "tools" to make him an outstanding player. He had the power to hit to all fields. He had an exceptional arm, and he was the fastest man on the team.

*Reggie's errors weren't all on the field during 1968, his first full season in the majors. Here, in a game against the Yankees, he finds himself picked off first base.*

Reggie tried hard in his first full season in the major leagues. Perhaps he tried too hard. He made some brilliant catches and throws. But he also played some singles into doubles, and occasionally allowed himself to be picked off base. He hit 29 home runs and drove in 74 runs. But he also made 18 errors, the highest total in the league that season, and struck out 171 times, the second highest total in baseball history.

With such a season, no one was prepared for what happened in 1969. Home run after home run boomed from Reggie's bat. By mid-June, he was well ahead of Babe Ruth's pace the year that Ruth hit 60 home runs.

Everywhere the A's played, Reggie was cheered on by the fans. There were stories about him in national magazines and in newspapers. His telephone never stopped ringing. He could not walk down a street without being recognized. He could not sit down in a restaurant without someone asking for his autograph. He had never gotten so much attention.

In a night game in Washington, D.C., Reggie blasted two home runs to lead the A's to a victory over the Washington Senators. President Richard M. Nixon was in the stands, and afterward Reggie

*Relaxing with a soft drink after hitting his 31st, 32nd, and 33rd home runs of the 1969 season in a game against Seattle.*

was asked how it felt to hit two home runs in front of the President. "Great!" said Reggie. "Just great!" Then he added, "Everyone knows who the President is; I wanted the President to know who Reggie Jackson is." The next day the President sent Reggie a letter acclaiming him for his home-run exploits.

By the end of July, Reggie had 40 home runs. He made up his mind that he would try to beat Ruth's record and also Roger Maris' mark of 61 homers for a 162-game season. Maybe he could hit 65 home runs, he thought, maybe even more. He began swinging for the fences on every pitch.

That was a mistake. Pitchers stopped throwing him fastballs and instead fed him curve balls off the plate. Sometimes an entire week would go by without Reggie seeing a good pitch. But he kept swinging. He swung at pitches over his head. He swung at pitches in the dirt. He missed most of them, and hit only seven homers in the last two months of the season.

Still, he wound up with 47 home runs, an exceptional total for a second-year player. He had a .275 batting average and drove in 118 runs. He was well satisfied.

*Reggie is congratulated by third-base coach, John McNamara, after cracking his 47th (and final) home run of the 1969 season.*

Year in and year out, the A's had always been close to the bottom in the American League's standings. In the decade beginning in 1958, they had never finished higher than sixth place. But in 1969, thanks mostly to Reggie's smoking bat, the A's ended up second. The years ahead seemed filled with promise.

Jim (Catfish) Hunter was becoming the main-

*Joe Rudi and Sal Bando, along with Reggie, gave the A's punch at the plate.*

stay of the Oakland pitching staff. Catfish was at his best when the chips were down. He had a perfect game to his credit, and had been a member of the American League's All-Star team in 1968. Jim (Blue Moon) Odom, a fireballing right-hander, was the team's No. 2 starter. The infield had capable Don Minchner at first base, and the cat-quick Campy Campaneris at shortstop. Sal Bando, the team's best long-ball hitter, was at third base. Bando and Reggie had been teammates at Arizona State. Dick Green was stationed at second base. Of Green, Reggie said, "He's the glue that holds the infield together."

During the 1969 season, the A's had brought up a young outfielder named Joe Rudi from their Des Moines (Iowa) farm team. Quiet and shy, Rudi was to quickly develop into the best left fielder in baseball and become Reggie's closest friend on the team.

Reggie felt that his fine season called for a raise in salary. He had earned $20,000 in 1969. He wanted $60,000 for 1970. Finley offered him $40,000.

Reggie decided to hold out until Finley met his demands. He refused to go to spring training. Eventually, a settlement was reached, with Reggie signing for about $46,000.

*Reggie and A's owner, Charles O. Finley, quarreled frequently during the 1970 season.*

But the experience made Reggie bitter. When he finally joined the team that year, he was quiet and moody. When he failed to get a hit, he would often throw his bat in a fit of anger or send his helmet clattering into the dugout.

Reggie began striking out frequently. His batting average sagged. He made errors in the field. The fans started booing him.

Finley ordered the manager to bench Reggie. That hurt. After a long stretch on the bench, Reggie was called on to pinch-hit, and slammed a homer with the bases loaded. As he rounded third and headed for home plate, Reggie looked up toward the box where Finley was seated, and raised his fist at the A's owner and shook it defiantly.

Finley was so angry, he announced that he might send Reggie back to the minor leagues. It would be good for him, said Finley.

The feuding with the A's owner was ruining Reggie's playing. He had trouble sleeping, and he began losing weight. He never dreamed that baseball would be like this, and he began to think about quitting.

Reggie realized that Finley was punishing him for holding out for a higher salary. "He wanted to break my spirit," Reggie says. "And he almost did."

Reggie had problems off the field, too. He had been married in 1969, but the marriage was not turning out well. "I was only 22 when I got married and I didn't know how to handle it," Reggie says. He and his wife separated. In 1973, they were divorced.

The dismal 1970 season finally ended. The A's finished second again, nine games behind the Minnesota Twins. Reggie's batting average tumbled to .237. He hit only 23 homers and drove in only 66 runs.

Reggie decided to play winter baseball in Puerto Rico. He joined the Santurce team, managed by Frank Robinson, another of his idols. Robinson, the only player in baseball to have been named the most valuable player in both leagues, was then a member of the Baltimore Orioles, American League champions in 1969.

Robinson spoke to Reggie as a father might speak to a son. "You're trying to do too much,"

*Says Reggie: "Frank Robinson taught me to control myself."*

he told him. "You can't expect to carry the whole club." Reggie had been given such advice before, but now it was coming from someone he admired and respected.

Reggie credits Robinson with teaching him "the most important thing in the world. . . . He taught me to control myself."

Reggie was a much improved player in 1971. He led the A's with 32 homers and 82 runs batted in. But the team's No. 1 celebrity that year was a young left-handed pitcher named Vida Blue. He threw the ball so hard that it came up to the plate

*Vida Blue, Oakland's brightest star in 1971.*

looking like an aspirin tablet. Blue finished with a 24-8 record, and he led the league with an 1.82 earned-run average.

Blue and Reggie were not the team's only stars. Catfish Hunter became a 20-game winner for the first time, and Sal Bando was an offensive standout with 24 homers and 94 runs batted in.

The A's wrapped up the division championship in mid-September, finishing six games ahead of the Kansas City Royals. They faced the Baltimore Orioles in the playoffs. It didn't seem to matter to the talented and experienced Orioles that the A's had Jackson, Bando, Blue and Hunter. Seeking their third consecutive pennant, they managed to overpower the Oakland team in three straight games.

The A's proved that they were no one-year fluke by winning the championship of their division a second time in 1972. Their strong pitching was again a key factor, although Vida Blue, who quarreled with Finley over contract terms throughout the early months of the season, won only six games. However, left-hander Ken Holtzman, obtained in a trade before the season had begun, took up the slack, recording 19 wins. Reggie and Joe Rudi were the offensive power of the team.

*Reggie was a sad figure following the A's defeat in the third game of the 1971 playoffs.*

In the playoff series against the Detroit Tigers, the A's won the first two games with ease. The Tigers won the third and fourth games. In the fifth and deciding contest, played at Tiger Stadium, Detroit took a 1-0 lead in the first inning.

The A's quickly answered back. With two outs in the second inning, and Reggie on third base and Mike Epstein on first, Manager Dick Williams called a delayed double steal. Epstein tore for second base. When Tiger catcher Bill Freehan fired the ball to shortstop Dick McAuliffe in an attempt to nip Epstein, Reggie exploded for home plate.

To prevent the run from scoring, McAuliffe grabbed the ball in front of second base, and whipped it back to Freehan. As Reggie shot down the basepath, he saw Freehan blocking the plate. Reggie hit the dirt. His slide sent Freehan sprawling. But suddenly Reggie felt a stab of pain. He reached for his leg and screamed in anguish. He had ripped a hamstring muscle.

*Reggie screams in pain as he injured his leg in stealing home in the deciding game of the 1972 playoffs.*

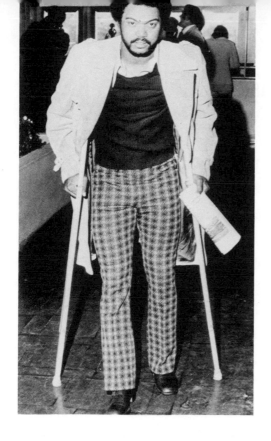

*For the 1972 World Series, Reggie was on crutches.*

Reggie lay on the ground and clutched his leg with both hands. His teammates streamed from the dugout and surrounded him. The fact that Reggie had scored the tying run was all but overlooked. When they helped Reggie from the field, his leg throbbed from his calf to the top of the thigh.

The A's went on to win that deciding playoff game, and then faced the powerful Cincinnati Reds in the World Series. Reggie's knee had been put in a cast and he got around on crutches. What should have been one of the most triumphant periods of his life — the realization of a boyhood dream: playing in a World Series — became one of the most unhappy for him. Dressed in street clothes, he watched the Series from the dugout.

The A's won in seven games. Reggie remembers the last out — Pete Rose flying deep to Joe Rudi in left-center field. The players went wild, yelling and screaming and throwing their arms about one another. As they came off the field, they seemed not to notice Reggie, and ran right by him into the clubhouse for their victory celebration.

Reggie's knee healed over the winter. As the 1973 season began, he went into every game with a winning attitude. To Reggie, winning is more than knowing what to do and when to do it. A winning player will do the job, no matter what. There can be no excuses.

Suppose there is a runner on first base, and no one out. The next batter's job is to advance that runner into scoring position. "It doesn't matter if the pitcher is right-handed or left-handed," Reggie says, "if he's throwing bullets or throwing curve balls off the top of the stadium. Nobody cares. Get the job done. Move the man into scoring position."

*A gifted fielder, Reggie ran from right field to the first-base fence to make this catch off the bat of Baltimore's Boog Powell during the season of 1973.*

37

*In 1973, Reggie clouted the longest ball ever hit at the Oakland Coliseum. It was retrieved by Bob Sannazzaro who returned the ball to Reggie.*

Reggie was never better than in 1973. He slammed a league-leading 32 home runs, including the longest home run ever hit in the Oakland Coliseum. It was a tremendous blast that landed in the top row of the right-field bleachers, 485 feet from home plate. Reggie also led the league in runs scored with 99 and in runs batted in with 117. His .293 batting average was the highest of his career.

The A's won their third successive division title, although they drew an unexpected challenge from Kansas City. The Royals stayed close until almost the final week of the season. The race ended with the A's winning by six games. This time the A's faced the Orioles in the playoffs. They struggled, but managed to tame the Baltimore team in five games.

While Oakland was wrapping up the pennant in the American League, the surprising New York Mets were doing the same in the National League. The Mets were a light hitting team and no better than average defensively. But what they did have was plenty of pitching. Right-handed Tom Seaver was the No. 1 hurler in the league. Close behind him was Jon Matlack, a hard-throwing left-hander. Jerry Koosman, another lefty, was a curve-ball pitcher. And there was no one better than Tug McGraw in coming out of the bullpen. It was McGraw who had made up the Mets' battlecry: "You gotta bee-leeeeve!"

The New York team went into the Series as underdogs, but they soon gave up that role. With the Series tied at two games apiece, Koosman spun a neat three-hitter to shut out the A's, 2-0, before wildly cheering fans at Shea Stadium. The

Oakland players were quiet on the plane back to home. They knew the Mets had to win only one more of the two remaining games. They also knew that the New Yorkers had Seaver and Matlack to do the job.

It had not been a good Series for Reggie. He was trying too hard. He was pressing. In the three games in New York, he had gotten just one hit. "A sleeping giant" one newspaper called him.

But Reggie awakened in the sixth game. With one out in the first inning and Tom Seaver pitch-

*Reggie catches Cleon Jones' sinking liner during 1973 World Series.*

ing, Joe Rudi singled. After Sal Bando went fishing for a sweeping curve and struck out, it was Reggie's turn. He belted Seaver's first pitch up the alley in left-center field for a long double. Rudi romped home with the game's first run.

Reggie was just beginning. With two out in the third inning, Bando lashed a Seaver fastball up the middle for a base hit. Then Reggie nailed the ball on a line into right center field. Rusty Staub, playing with a bad right shoulder, threw weakly to the cutoff man, and Bando sprinted home. Again Reggie wound up on second base.

That made the score 2-0 in Oakland's favor. Meanwhile, Catfish Hunter was stopping the Mets cold.

Reggie wasn't finished for the day. In the eighth inning, he smacked a line-drive single into center field. Don Hahn mishandled the ball, and by the time he got it back into the infield, Reggie was standing on third base. Soon after, he scored on a sacrifice fly. The A's won, 3-1, to even the Series.

The final game was played at the Oakland Coliseum on a warm and sunny afternoon. Jon Matlack went to the mound for the Mets. The A's countered with Ken Holtzman.

Matlack started to unravel in the third inning. Campy Campaneris homered to shoot the A's into a 2-0 lead. After Rudi singled, Bando popped up, bringing Reggie to the plate. The count went to one-and-one. Matlack glanced at first, then let loose a curve ball — but it hung. Reggie whipped his bat into the ball and sent it sailing into the right field seats.

Reggie circled the bases, grinning all the way. And when he reached home plate, he jumped on it with both feet. It was the decisive blow in Oakland's 5-2 win.

*Reggie's home run in the seventh game of the 1973 World Series boosted the A's into a 4-0 lead.*

It was an outstanding Series for Reggie Jackson. He had batted .310 against the famed Met pitching, knocking in six runs and scoring three runs. The clubhouse celebration was in full swing when Reggie was told that he had been named the Most Valuable Player in the Series. It made him feel proud. "In the World Series, all the marbles are on the line," Reggie said. "It's like saying, 'Okay big fella, you had a big year, you're a star. But can you do it *now*?' I did."

Not long after, Reggie was named the American League's Most Valuable Player for the 1973 season. He was the No. 1 choice of every writer who voted. Only five other American League players had ever been unanimous choices in the MVP balloting.

Following the World Series, Dick Williams, the Oakland manager, had quit. To replace him, Finley hired Alvin Dark, who had been a fine shortstop with the New York Giants in the 1950s. Dark had managed the A's before, in 1966 and 1967.

The A's had now been world champions two years in a row. Winning three straight was not going to be an easy task, they knew. In fact, only twice before in baseball history had a team won

*Alvin Dark (on bench) took over as A's manager in 1974.*

as many as three consecutive World Series. The New York Yankees won four in a row (1936-1939) and five in a row (1949-1953).

Reggie began the 1974 season with the hottest bat of his career. Through the first eight weeks he hit at a .399 clip; he had 15 home runs and 42 runs batted in. *Sports Illustrated* called him a "super-duperstar."

Reggie's popularity soared to a new high. In the All-Star balloting, he received a record 3,497,358 votes, almost a million more than the runner-up vote getter, Hank Aaron.

But the season had its bad moments, too. One afternoon the A's were playing the Cleveland Indians. Oakland center fielder Bill North, known for his moodiness, led off the game by hitting the ball back to the pitcher and not running it out. When he came back to the dugout, Reggie glared at him and said, "Hey, man, what's wrong? Don't you feel good or what?"

North said he was feeling fine.

"Then why didn't you run that ball out?" Reggie asked.

North scowled. "What business is it of yours?" he said. "Until you have 'Mgr.' after your name, butt out of my business." Then North stormed off.

*Reggie and teammate Gene Tenace prepare to take the field against the New York Yankees during 1974 season.*

In the weeks that followed, North became increasingly bitter, and began to needle Reggie. Finally, the two became involved in a clubhouse fight. Reggie lunged at North, slipped, and fell against a metal locker. Their teammates pulled them apart. But Reggie had injured his shoulder.

Although he continued to play, he could no longer swing the bat normally because of the shoulder injury. Later in the season, he injured a hamstring muscle sliding into third base, and had to sit out several games. His batting average slipped and his run production fell. He ended up hitting only .289 and his home run total never got above 29.

*Early in the 1974 season, Reggie collided with Bill North. Neither was hurt. Later on, they brawled in the clubhouse.*

*Injuries plagued Reggie during 1974. Here, accompanied by the A's trainer, he leaves the field after hurting his leg sliding into third base.*

Despite Reggie's weakened bat, the A's had little trouble winning their fourth straight division championship. Then they crushed the Orioles in four games in the playoffs.

In the National League, the Los Angeles Dodgers won the pennant. Since the World Series opponents were both from California, it was called the Freeway Series, the first in baseball history.

The Dodgers had impressive pitching in Andy Messersmith and Don Sutton, both right-handers. Messersmith, a 20-game winner in 1974, was a hard thrower with a fine change-up that kept batters off-stride. Sutton, a sinker-ball specialist, had won 19 games. They were backed up by Mike Marshall. When he was right, Marshall was the best reliever in baseball.

The first game was played under bright sunshine before 55,974 fans, a record crowd for Dodger Stadium. Ken Holtzman faced Andy Messersmith.

The huge crowd, the hundreds of press, radio, and television representatives, the drama of the opening game — it all excited Reggie and he could hardly wait to take his turn at bat.

Batting clean-up, Reggie faced Messersmith to open the second inning. The count went to one-and-one. Messersmith stared in for the sign. Reggie waited, his feet wide apart, the bat cocked.

Messersmith's pitch was a slider, high, at about Reggie's shoulders. Reggie took an awesome cut. The ball sprang from his bat and traveled like a cannon shot toward left field. As he started to run, Reggie watched the ball. He saw it keep rising until it cleared the outfield barrier to land in the seats. Then he saw the fans scrambling for it. Reggie grinned from ear to ear as he circled the bases.

The A's went on to win the game, 3-2. But the Dodgers squared matters in the second game behind Don Sutton. The Series then moved to Oakland. Catfish Hunter went to the mound for the A's, and captured his fifth straight victory in World Series competition, although he needed relief from Rollie Fingers. Now the A's led, two games to one.

In the fourth game, played at night, the Dodgers called upon Andy Messersmith once more. Messersmith was working with a 2-1 lead when the A's came to bat in the sixth inning. Lead-off man Bill North walked. When Messersmith tried to pick him off first base, his throw was wild, and North scampered to second. Sal Bando singled to drive him home with the tying run.

Now it was Reggie's turn to bat. Since his home run in the first game, the Dodger pitchers had been wary of him, and he seldom saw a good pitch. This turn at bat was typical, and Reggie walked.

When Joe Rudi laid down a perfect sacrifice bunt, Reggie sped into second base; Bando took third. Rookie Claudell Washington was purposely passed to load the bases.

Pinch-hitter Jim Holt then lashed the ball into right field, and it dropped in front of outfielder Joe Ferguson. Bando ran for home with the tie-breaking run. Reggie put his head down and raced for third. He rounded the base as Ferguson fired toward home plate.

Pounding toward home, Reggie could see catcher Steve Yeager waiting for the ball. It came in a little to Yeager's right. He reached for the ball, gloved it, and then adjusted his feet to block the plate. Reggie saw Sal Bando signaling for him to slide.

Reggie slid, sticking his right foot between Yeager's legs and across the plate. Yeager lunged at him with the ball, but missed. "Safe! Safe! He's safe!" Reggie heard Sal Bando screeching. Then he looked at the umpire who was signaling that he had made it.

Sure that he had made the tag, Yeager exploded, screaming at the umpire. It was now 4-2 in favor of the A's. They went on to win, 5-2.

It was a crucial victory for the A's. If they had lost, the Series would have been tied. But now, leading three games to one, they appeared un-

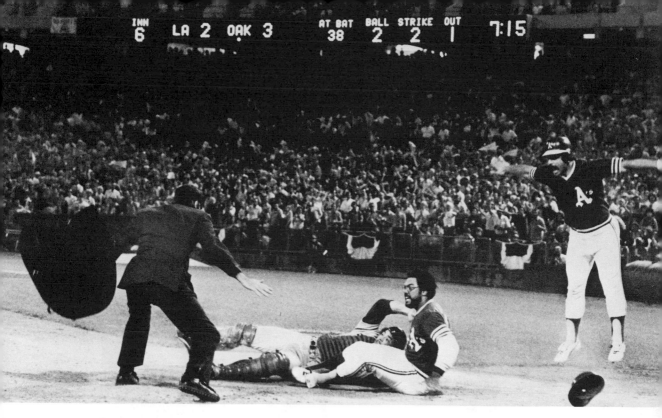

*Safe at home in the fourth game of the 1974 World Series. Steve Yeager is the Dodger catcher.*

beatable. "There is no way this team is going to lose now," Reggie said.

The Dodgers were not dead, however. In the fifth game, the A's were leading, 3-2, after seven innings of play, when L.A.'s Bill Buckner hit one of Rollie Fingers' pitches into right center field. Buckner rounded first base, and when he saw the ball bounce past Bill North, he kept right on running, making the turn at second base and heading for third.

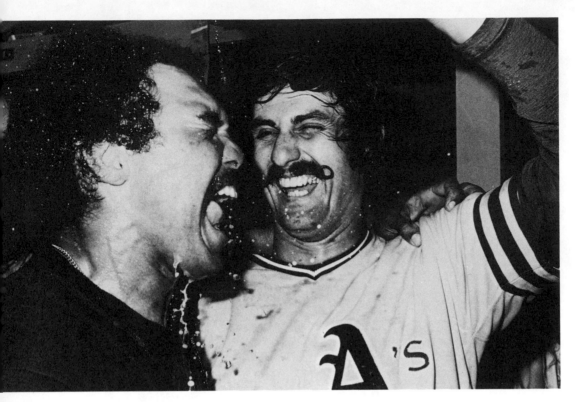

*Reggie celebrates with Rollie Fingers following Oakland's win of the 1974 World Series.*

Backing up the play, Reggie fielded the ball cleanly and in the same motion fired a strike to Dick Green, the relay man. Green uncorked a perfect throw to Sal Bando at third base. When Buckner slid into third, Bando had the ball and was waiting for him. He tagged Buckner hard. It wasn't even close.

The play dashed Dodger hopes. They did not threaten again.

With the final out, hysterical Oakland fans poured out onto the field, trying to reach the players. Reggie had to struggle to get to the clubhouse. By the time he entered, the celebration was already in progress.

The A's had now been crowned world champions three times in a row. Could they win four straight championships? Their chances were reduced when it became known that Catfish Hunter, who had won 161 games in his ten years with the team, was leaving. When Finley had failed to fulfill certain provisions in Hunter's contract, he was declared a free agent, and given the right to sign with the highest bidder. He would be joining the New York Yankees.

While the A's did manage to win the division crown in 1975, they were upset in the playoffs by

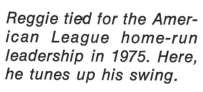

*Reggie tied for the American League home-run leadership in 1975. Here, he tunes up his swing.*

the Boston Red Sox. The Boston team, sparked by their two phenomenal rookies, Fred Lynn and Jim Rice, outplayed the A's from the opening pitch.

Before the 1976 season opened, the world of baseball was shaken when the courts decided that players, once their contracts had expired,

*Reggie twists himself into a pretzel in swinging at a pitch and missing during the 1975 playoff series, won by the Boston Red Sox.*

would be free to shop around among other teams. Previously, the baseball contract said that a player had to stay with one team for as long as he played.

Reggie decided to take advantage of the new ruling. His contract expired at the end of the 1976 season, and he would look for employment with another team.

But Finley, aware of what Reggie was going to do, had his own plan. Not long before the 1976 season opened, he traded Jackson to the Baltimore Orioles. Pitcher Ken Holtzman also went to the Baltimore team as part of the trade. In return, the A's received outfielder Don Baylor and pitchers Mike Torrez and Paul Mitchell.

Upon learning that Reggie was leaving, Sal Bando said, "A guy grows on you when you've been around each other for so long. It's going to be quiet around the batting cage without him. I just can't help but be saddened."

Reggie himself was not so much saddened as he was shocked. He didn't like the idea of leaving the West Coast, of leaving his friends, his home, and his business interests. He refused to join his new team.

Part of the problem was financial. Reggie wanted a raise in salary. It was rumored that he and the Orioles finally agreed on around $200,000, although the actual figure was never revealed.

Although Reggie agreed to the financial terms, he did not sign a contract with the Orioles. By not signing, he would become a free agent at the end of the season.

The season was a month old by the time Reggie finally joined the Orioles. A crowd of 24,805 turned out for his first appearance with the team. When he came to the plate in the second inning, they gave him a roaring ovation. Ironically, Reggie's old teammates, the A's, were the opposing team. Reggie went hitless in two official trips to the plate, but when he grounded out in the sixth inning, he drove in the tying run in a game the Orioles won.

The Orioles were in next to last place in the Eastern Division of the American League when Reggie joined the team. They soon began an upward climb, thanks in part to his contributions. His first home run was a bases-loaded smash that enabled the Orioles to beat Milwaukee. Two days later, he touched off a two-run rally against Catfish Hunter to spark another Baltimore win.

Reggie began hitting more often in June. By August, despite his late start, he ranked among

*In joining the Orioles, Reggie left his home and friends on the West Coast, but brought his big bat wtih him.*

the league leaders in home runs and runs batted in.

But the Orioles as a team had their ups and downs. They would win six or seven games in a row, then lose just as many. They managed to get as high as second place in the standings, but could go no higher.

At the end of November that year, baseball staged what was called its "free-agent reentry draft." A total of 24 players were put up for auction. Many of them were former teammates of Reggie's. His good friend Joe Rudi was to sign with the California Angels. Sal Bando accepted an offer from the Milwaukee Braves. Rollie Fingers went to the San Diego Padres, and Campy Campaneris to the Texas Rangers.

Reggie still had not signed a contract with the Orioles. And day by day, guessing increased as to which team he would choose. The Montreal Expos, San Diego Padres, and New York Yankees were the teams that wanted him the most. Reggie took his time making up his mind, weighing each of the offers carefully. Finally, he agreed to accept the Yankees' offer. It amounted to almost $3 million for five years. Reggie's decision was not based on money alone. Other teams had offered him more. But he liked New York, the city's color and excitement. Being the headquarters for the television networks was a factor, too. Reggie had ambitions of being a television personality one day.

George Steinbrenner, the Yankee owner, was still another factor. "He dealt with me as a man and a person," Reggie said. "I feel that I'm a friend of his."

Reggie called the Yankees "the best team in

baseball." Few people were willing to argue this fact with him. The New York pitching staff featured two of Reggie's former Oakland teammates, Catfish Hunter and Ken Holtzman, the last-named obtained from the Orioles during the summer of 1976.

Yankee catching was the best in baseball, for behind the plate they boasted Thurman Munson, the American League's Most Valuable Player of 1976. At third base was Graig Nettles, the league's leading home-run hitter that year. First base was manned by clutch-hitting Chris Chambliss.

Reggie would be joining an outfield that included Roy White and Mickey Rivers. White was one of the most underrated players in the game; Rivers, one of the speediest. Some sports writers said that the Yankees might be American League champions for years to come.

They began living up to expectations right away, winning the American League title in 1977, Reggie's first year with the team. They then faced the heavily favored Dodgers in the World Series.

In the third game, Reggie scored the winning run in the fourth inning. He hit a home run in the fourth game, and another in the fifth game on his last trip to the plate.

The Yankees went into the sixth game leading 3 games to 2. One more victory and they would be world champions.

In the fourth inning, with the Dodgers ahead, 3-2, and Munson on first base, Reggie drove the first pitch on a line into the right field stands. Next inning, he lined the first pitch into the right field stands again.

Reggie was not finished. Leading off in the eighth inning, he cracked the first pitch in the center field stands, the ball traveling on a great soaring arc to land 450 feet away from home plate. The fans went wild. The Yankees won, 8-4 — and the World Series.

Three swings — three home runs! Four consecutive home runs and five home runs in one series! No one had ever seen a championship performance like that before. So great was his popularity, that a candy bar was named after him—*Reggie!*

The 1978 season got off to a gloomy beginning. Reggie was not playing like his old self. He quarreled often with manager Billy Martin, as did other players.

*Jackson's home-run heroics earned him this salute from the Yankee Stadium scoreboard.*

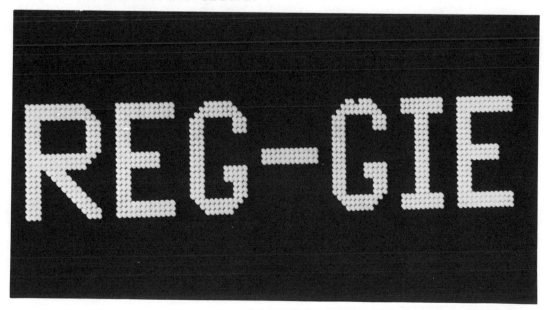

The Yanks fell 14 games behind the league-leading Red Sox.

Then Martin was replaced by easy-going Bob Lemon. Reggie's bat began to boom again, and the Yankees started winning. The season ended in a tie, which meant just one playoff game to decide the winner of the American League's Eastern Division. The Yanks whipped the Red Sox, and went on to bury Kansas City in the championship playoffs.

In the World Series against the Los Angeles Dodgers, Reggie drummed out one key hit after another. Again the Dodgers fell to the Yankees. For his clutch hitting in the playoffs and the World Series, sportswriters began calling Reggie "Mr. October."

As a boy growing up, Reggie collected baseball cards. He had several cigar boxes full of them. Sometimes he would go through his collection, examining the cards one by one. "All those great players, come and gone," he would think to himself. "They didn't get much time, but they left a mark."

That's what Reggie dreamed of doing, if he ever were to become a major league player. He dreamed of leaving a mark, of being remembered. As one of baseball's all-time greats, he has surely succeeded.

# REGGIE JACKSON

**Born: May 18, 1946 at Wyncote, Pennsylvania**
**Height: 6'          Weight: 204 lbs.**

## REGULAR SEASON

| Year | Team | League | G | AB | R | H | 2B | 3B | HR | RBI | Pct. |
|------|------|--------|---|----|----|---|----|----|----|-----|------|
| 1966 | Lewiston | Northwest | 12 | 48 | 14 | 14 | 3 | 2 | 2 | 11 | .292 |
| 1966 | Modesto | California | 56 | 221 | 50 | 66 | 6 | 0 | 21 | 60 | .299 |
| 1967 | Birmingham | Southern | 114 | 413 | 84 | 121 | 26 | 17 | 17 | 58 | .293 |
| 1967 | Kansas City | American | 35 | 118 | 13 | 21 | 4 | 4 | 1 | 6 | .178 |
| 1968 | Oakland | American | 154 | 553 | 82 | 138 | 13 | 6 | 29 | 74 | .250 |
| 1969 | Oakland | American | 152 | 549 | 123 | 151 | 36 | 3 | 47 | 118 | .275 |
| 1970 | Oakland | American | 149 | 426 | 57 | 101 | 21 | 2 | 23 | 66 | .237 |
| 1971 | Oakland | American | 150 | 567 | 87 | 157 | 29 | 3 | 32 | 80 | .277 |
| 1972 | Oakland | American | 135 | 499 | 72 | 132 | 25 | 2 | 25 | 75 | .265 |
| 1973 | Oakland | American | 151 | 539 | 99 | 158 | 28 | 2 | 32 | 117 | .293 |
| 1974 | Oakland | American | 148 | 506 | 90 | 146 | 25 | 1 | 29 | 93 | .289 |
| 1975 | Oakland | American | 157 | 593 | 91 | 150 | 39 | 3 | 36 | 104 | .253 |
| 1976 | Baltimore | American | 134 | 498 | 84 | 138 | 27 | 2 | 27 | 91 | .277 |
| 1977 | New York | American | 146 | 525 | 93 | 150 | 39 | 2 | 32 | 110 | .286 |
| 1978 | New York | American | 139 | 511 | 82 | 140 | 13 | 5 | 27 | 97 | .274 |

## ALL-STAR GAME

| Year | League | AB | R | H | 2B | 3B | HR | RBI | Pct. |
|------|--------|----|----|----|----|----|----|-----|------|
| 1969 | American | 2 | 0 | 0 | 0 | 0 | 0 | 0 | .000 |
| 1971 | American | 1 | 1 | 1 | 0 | 0 | 1 | 2 | 1.000 |
| 1972 | American | 4 | 0 | 2 | 1 | 0 | 0 | 0 | .500 |
| 1973 | American | 4 | 1 | 1 | 1 | 0 | 0 | 0 | .250 |
| 1974 | American | 3 | 0 | 0 | 0 | 0 | 0 | 0 | .000 |
| 1975 | American | 3 | 0 | 1 | 0 | 0 | 0 | 0 | .333 |
| 1977 | American | 2 | 0 | 1 | 0 | 0 | 0 | 0 | .500 |
| 1978 | American | | | | (withdrew) | | | | |

## CHAMPIONSHIP PLAYOFFS

| Year | Team | League | G | AB | R | H | 2B | 3B | HR | RBI | Pct. |
|------|------|--------|---|----|----|----|----|----|----|-----|------|
| 1971 | Oakland | American | 3 | 12 | 2 | 4 | 1 | 0 | 2 | 2 | .333 |
| 1972 | Oakland | American | 5 | 18 | 1 | 5 | 1 | 0 | 0 | 2 | .278 |
| 1973 | Oakland | American | 5 | 21 | 0 | 3 | 0 | 0 | 0 | 0 | .143 |
| 1974 | Oakland | American | 4 | 12 | 0 | 2 | 1 | 0 | 0 | 1 | .167 |
| 1975 | Oakland | American | 3 | 12 | 1 | 5 | 0 | 0 | 1 | 3 | .417 |
| 1977 | New York | American | 5 | 16 | 1 | 2 | 0 | 0 | 0 | 1 | .125 |
| 1978 | New York | American | 4 | 13 | 5 | 6 | 1 | 0 | 2 | 6 | .461 |

## WORLD SERIES

| Year | Team | League | G | AB | R | H | 2B | 3B | HR | RBI | Pct. |
|------|------|--------|---|----|----|----|----|----|----|-----|------|
| 1972 | Oakland | American | (Injured, did not play) | | | | | | | | |
| 1973 | Oakland | American | 7 | 29 | 3 | 9 | 3 | 1 | 1 | 6 | .310 |
| 1974 | Oakland | American | 5 | 14 | 3 | 4 | 1 | 0 | 1 | 1 | .286 |
| 1977 | New York | American | 6 | 20 | 10 | 9 | 1 | 0 | 5 | 8 | .450 |
| 1978 | New York | American | 6 | 23 | 2 | 9 | 1 | 0 | 2 | 8 | .391 |